ANIMALS MATE

A Book About Where Babies Come From

EMILY FARRANTO

For Oscar and Ivan, of course.

Published by Familius LLC, www.familius.com
1254 Commerce Way, Sanger, CA 93657

Familius books are available at special discounts for bulk purchases, whether
for sales promotions or for family or corporate use. For more information,
contact Familius Sales at 559-876-2170 or email orders@familius.com.

Library of Congress Control Number: 2019956743

Print ISBN 9781641702454
Ebook ISBN 9781641703093

Printed in China

Edited by Brooke Jorden and Deb Greenberg
Cover design by Carlos Guerrero and Brooke Jorden
Book design by Brooke Jorden

10 9 8 7 6 5 4 3 2 1

First Edition

This is a book about
animals mating.

Mating is when two animals come together to reproduce.

Reproduce means to make
a new living thing.

Sexual reproduction is when a male and female
come together to produce a new
living thing—in other words, a baby.

Sheep make sheep babies.

Hedgehogs make
hedgehog babies.

Beluga whales make
beluga whale babies.

Most animals, including humans, reproduce.

Animals mate and reproduce
once they are adults.

The female animal has a tiny *egg* inside of her, and the male animal has something called *sperm* inside of him.

Sperm goes through his penis into the female's vagina to join the egg.

The egg is *fertilized*, which means a baby begins to grow, or in some cases, many babies.

Frogs and many kinds of fish sexually reproduce, but fertilization happens outside the body, in the water.

After the animals mate, the eggs
are fertilized and grow into babies.

The time it takes for babies to be
born is called *gestation*.

After gestation, when they are ready
to live in the world, the babies are born—
or in some cases, hatch from eggs.

Marsupials—koalas, for example—are a little different.

The baby grows inside the mother, and then she gives birth when the baby is *almost* but not quite ready to live in the world.

The baby is born and then grows a little more in a pouch on the mother's body.

A lot of animals mate only during certain seasons, but some mate year-round.

When the animal is an adult and
ready to reproduce, instincts tell the
animal more about when and how
mating works.

If you see two lovebugs
together like this . . .

or two snails together like this . . .

or two turtles together like this . . .
they are probably mating.

Mating is an interesting part of nature.

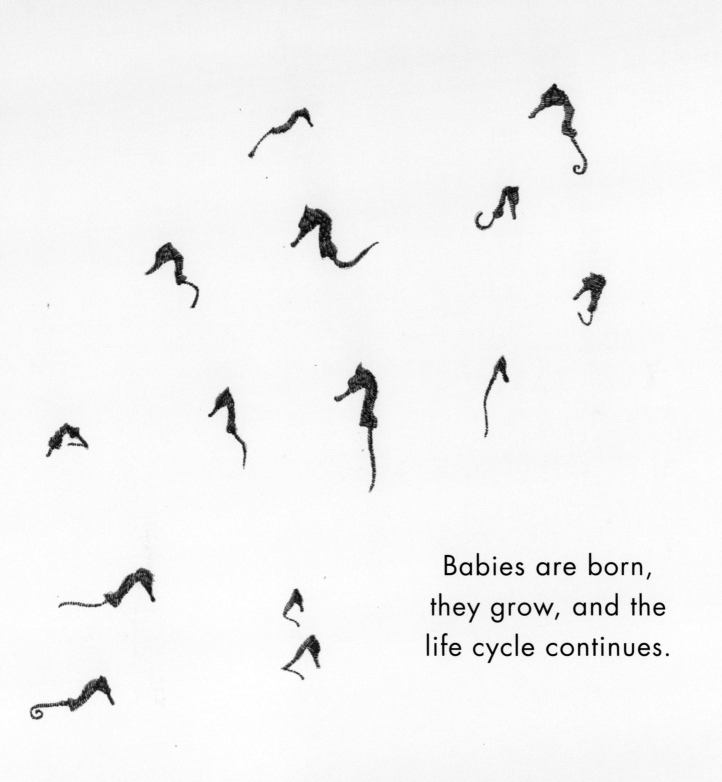

Babies are born,
they grow, and the
life cycle continues.

A Note to Parents

This book is the result of a question my son asked me when he was about six years old. He knew that part of a man and part of a woman came together to make a baby. Sooner than I would have thought, he wanted to know more. I had three choices: I could lie, avoid, or answer. I chose to answer.

I made the first set of these drawings to use as a focal point for our discussion. I left the drawings out in our living room, in our family's common space, so that it was my son who approached me and not the other way around. I recommend the same approach with the book, that it not be presented as a gift, but left around to be asked about or reached for when the question is posed.

When my son asked about the drawings, I made sure to keep my voice and body-language neutral, not over-eager, and to mirror his level of interest. I suggest reading this book the same way. The text briefly mentions humans, answering the question of where babies come from. It states that reproduction happens between adults. Then, focus shifts back to the animals. After that first conversation with my son, he had learned simply what every child living on a farm knows early on. My hope is that this book will help answer your child's early questions without breaching personal boundaries or boundaries of age-appropriateness. This gentle and factual explanation can be given to children in any type of family from any type of background.

This book aims to serve as the opening of a dialogue and the setting of a tone. It can be a catalyst for healthy conversation and honest answers, and can help children learn these most basic facts prior to becoming self-conscious about asking. I hope your child will continue to come to you with questions and your shared knowledge, rooted in nature and honesty, will make more complicated questions that touch on culture and morality easier to answer according to your family's values.

This book aims to advocate for the most important family value: I am here for you. Ask me.

—EF